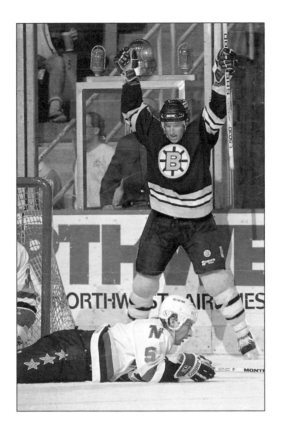

CREATIVE EDUCATION

BOSTON

BRUINS

VARTAN KUPELIAN

Published by Creative Education
123 South Broad Street, Mankato, Minnesota 56001
Creative Education is an imprint of The Creative Company

Designed by Rita Marshall
Cover Illustration by Rob Day

Photos by: Bettmann Archives, Bruce Bennett Studios, Focus on Sports,
Protography, Spectra Action and Wide World Photos

Library of Congress Cataloging-in-Publication Data

Kupelian, Vartan.
Boston Bruins / Vartan Kupelian.
p. cm. — (NHL Today)
ISBN 0-88682-669-1

1. Boston Bruins (Hockey team)—History—Juvenile literature.
[1. Boston Bruins (Hockey team)—History. 2. Hockey—History.]
I. Title. II. Series.

GV848.B6K86   1995   93-48437
796.962'64'0974461—dc20

123456

CRADLE OF DEFENSEMEN: FROM SHORE TO ORR

"The Goal" is etched forever in the minds of hockey fans everywhere. Like a masterpiece, it is timeless, as revered today as it was more than two decades ago.

In the spring of 1970, the Boston Bruins were on the verge of winning their first Stanley Cup in 29 years. They were up three games to none against the expansion St. Louis Blues. It was only a matter of time before the magic moment when the Bruins would officially celebrate their long-awaited triumph.

Cecil "Tiny" Thompson was one of the Bruins' first stars.

Art Ross coached the first-year team to a 6-24-0 win-loss-tie record.

Little did anyone know what the great Bobby Orr had in store to cap the occasion. The Bruins, on veteran Johnny Bucyk's third-period goal, had rallied to tie the game 3-3 and send it into overtime, meaning they were just one goal away from the coveted Stanley Cup. The underdog Blues knew they would be facing an irresistible force—the most potent offense in hockey, spearheaded by the dynamic Orr. Even so, nobody could have anticipated the suddenness with which the Bruins would strike. They needed just 40 seconds of overtime to end it.

Once the puck was dropped at center ice, Orr took over. He led a rush into the St. Louis zone, beat a defender and skated straight for the net. Derek Sanderson, another of the Bruins' young guns, sent the speeding Orr a perfect pass. The puck and the player arrived at the same instant and Orr shot. Goal!

The images of Orr's remarkable effort, captured on film, show him flying triumphantly through the air in celebration of the historic goal. The photos were reproduced in newspapers and magazines wherever hockey is played. It is among the sport's most enduring memories.

It was fitting that the man who ended the Bruins' championship drought with such a dramatic goal was Orr, a defenseman. After all, Boston is "the Cradle of Defensemen." The trend began with the great Eddie Shore, Aubrey "Dit" Clapper, Lionel Hitchman and Albert "Babe" Siebert in the 1920s and 1930s and has continued through the years with such outstanding defensemen as Ferny Flaman, Bill Quackenbush, Leo Boivin, Tom Johnson and Brad Park. Hockey's modern era produced the incomparable Orr.

Boston has won the Stanley Cup, symbolic of the NHL championship, five times in its history. The team's rise and fall over

Bobby Orr scored six consecutive 100-or-more point seasons (page 7).

nearly seven decades can be traced to the men on defense. They are the embodiment of the Bruins.

1 9 3 2

Eddie Shore won his first of four consecutive Hart Trophies as the league's MVP.

THE EDMONTON EXPRESS

The Bruins' home city is the capital of Massachusetts. It is located in the eastern part of the state, on an arm of the Atlantic Ocean called Boston Bay. An important city during the American Revolution, Boston remains the spiritual capital of New England and is a hub for educational, financial, cultural and medical activities.

Not surprisingly, Boston has long been a hotbed of sports. Its major professional teams include basketball's Celtics, baseball's Red Sox, football's Patriots—and, of course, hockey's Bruins, the oldest National Hockey League franchise in the United States.

The team began in 1924, when Charles F. Adams, a millionaire sportsman from Boston, was granted the franchise. Hoping to establish an identity for his team, he decided that the team's name should relate to an untamed brown animal of "size, strength, agility, ferocity and cunning." In a name-the-team contest, the winning selection was Bruin, meaning bear.

Arthur Howey Ross was hired as the first general manager and coach. For 30 seasons, from 1924 to 1953, Ross helped mold the Boston Bruins into a tough, competitive team. He also made many contributions to the game of hockey itself, including the loose-mesh goal net, the beveled-edged hockey puck and various coaching strategies. The Art Ross Trophy, which honors the league's leading scorer, is named after him.

During their inaugural season, the Boston Bruins won only six of 30 games, but the team's fortunes took a swift turn the following season with the arrival of a young man from Saskatchewan named Eddie Shore. Shore was a powerful man whose nicknames included "the Edmonton Express." He skated fast and hard and possessed a mean streak that frightened opponents. His unique combination of toughness and ability made him the most respected player of his time and a forerunner of the "Big, Bad Bruins" style of hockey that has characterized the Boston team over the years. For 13 seasons he dominated the NHL, winning the Hart Trophy as the most valuable player four times and being named to the All-Star team seven times.

Behind Dit Clapper (#5) and Bill Cowley (#10), the Bruins won their second Stanley Cup in three years.

"When Shore carried the puck you were always sure something would happen," said Boston trainer Hammy Moore.

And so it was that the Shore era included one of the most famous on-ice incidents in NHL history. It happened during a Boston-Toronto game on December 12, 1933, at Boston Garden, home of the Bruins.

Shore, angry at being tripped by a Toronto player, set out on a rink-long dash to retaliate. The first opposing player he encountered was Ace Bailey. Shore hit him from behind and flipped him over. The sheer force of the blow sent Bailey crashing to the ice, where he lay unconscious. Shore himself suffered a concussion when Bailey's teammate, Red Horner, punched him in the face in reprisal. The crowd sat stunned. For days, while Bailey lay in a Boston hospital with a serious head injury, his life hanging in the balance, the incident made front-page headlines in newspapers across the United States and Canada.

After a series of delicate operations, Bailey recovered, but his hockey career was over. Shore was suspended for six weeks. At the end of the season, he played in what was to become the NHL's first All-Star Game. It was in the form of a benefit

John Bucyk is the Bruins' top scorer of all-time.

Derek Sanderson won the NHL Calder Trophy in 1967 68.

for Bailey. Before the game, Shore skated across the ice to where Bailey was sitting in Toronto's Maple Leaf Gardens. As everybody watched anxiously, Shore held out his hand.

"I'm sorry Ace," he said. "Forgive me."

Bailey shook his hand warmly, bringing to an end one of hockey's greatest dramas.

Frank Brimsek won his second Vezina Trophy as the NHL's top goaltender.

PEAKS AND VALLEYS

With Shore leading the way, the Bruins were one of the elite teams in the league in the late 1920s and 1930s. They captured the Stanley Cup in 1929, storming past the Montreal Canadiens and the New York Rangers. In the years that followed, they continued to be strong contenders for the

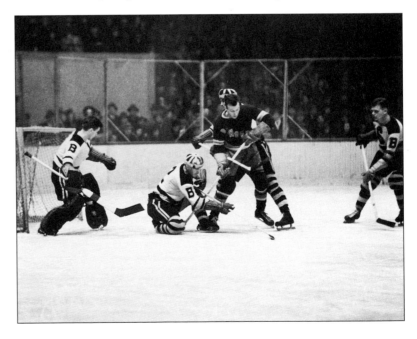

Cup, but weren't able to claim ultimate victory again until 1939, when they defeated Toronto.

The 1939 championship team included one of the most famous lines in league history—Milt Schmidt, Woody Dumart and Bobby Bauer—and stalwarts such as Bill Cowley and Bill "Flash" Hollett. The goaltender was Frankie Brimsek, known as "Mr. Zero." Another stalwart was Aubrey "Dit" Clapper, who played on three Stanley Cup teams. "Dit" was Clapper's childhood variation of his given name, Aubrey Victor. "I couldn't say Vic," Clapper explained. "I'd lisp the name and it came out Dit. It stuck."

Clapper was an even-tempered man who gave up lacrosse to pursue a hockey career, signing his first pro contract with the Bruins as a 19-year-old in 1926. Originally a defenseman, Clapper was converted to forward, where he joined Ralph Weiland and Dutch Gainor to make up what became known as Boston's "Dynamite Line." After 10 years as a forward, he switched back to defense, where he starred for 10 more seasons. He was an All-Star six times during his career and played on more Stanley Cup championship teams than any player in Bruins history. In 1945 Clapper became the first active player enshrined in the Hall of Fame.

Boston won the Stanley Cup again in 1941, this time against Detroit. But for the next 26 seasons, the Bruins made the finals only four times: in 1946, 1953, 1957 and 1958. Each time, however, they were defeated by the league-dominating Montreal Canadiens.

During that period, the competitive Milt Schmidt was the link to the Bruins' successful past. Schmidt was only 17 when he joined the Bruins in the early 1940s, but over the years, he became their inspirational leader. His playing days came to an

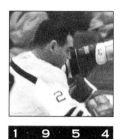

1 · 9 · 5 · 4

Hall of Fame defenseman Leo Boivin was one of the early greats for the Bruins.

end after the 1953 season, but he took over as coach from 1962 to 1966 and as general manager from 1967 to 1972.

Among the leaders of the club Schmidt inherited were Fern Flaman, Bronco Horvath, Vic Stasiuk and Johnny Bucyk. Bucyk made a lasting contribution, wearing the gold and black for 21 straight years. By the time he retired in 1978, he held numerous Boston career records, including most goals (545), most assists (794) and most consecutive games (418).

But even with Bucyk the Bruins struggled. The club was made up mostly of aging veterans and young draft selections who had failed to develop. Between the 1959–60 and 1966–67 seasons, the team finished fifth twice and sixth six times—in a league of only six teams. Bruins fans began looking for a player to give them hope. And as it turned out, that player's name was Bobby Orr.

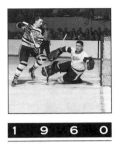

1 9 6 0

Don McKenney won the NHL Lady Byng Trophy for his sportsmanship and playing ability.

"WONDER BOY"

Few sportsmen in history have left such an imprint on their game as Bobby Orr, the man who revolutionized hockey.

Orr grew up in the little town of Parry Sound, Ontario, 140 miles north of Toronto on beautiful Georgian Bay. As a 14-year-old he often played against grown men. A Bruins scout discovered Orr and eventually talked his parents into letting the young phenom play on a junior team in Oshawa. Playing in Oshawa meant the Bruins, who sponsored the team, gained Orr's professional rights.

The Bruins signed Orr to a two-year, $75,000 contract, an unheard-of figure for a teenage rookie in those days, and he

Goaltender Andy Moog protects the Boston goal (page 15).

played his first NHL game in 1966. Early in his career, he wore his blonde hair in a crewcut, which made him look more like a choirboy than a superstar in the tough, hard-hitting game of hockey. His nicknames included "Wonder Boy" and "Super child." But when he put on his skates, there was no mistaking him for anything but the best player in hockey.

Before Orr's arrival, defensemen rarely ventured into offensive roles. A defenseman's job was to prevent goals, not score. But Orr was such a dynamic player and breathtaking skater that it was difficult—by design or by accident—to limit his game. He was impossible to contain.

"When Bobby Orr had the puck, he could do anything he wanted on a whim," said Brad Park, another Bruins defense-

1 9 7 2

Gerry Cheevers set the team record for longest unbeaten streak by a goaltender.

16

John McKenzie added scoring power to the front line.

man in the Hall of Fame. "From all the players I saw in their primes, he was the best ever for just taking control of a game, dominating it."

Terry O'Reilly (#24) and Phil Esposito (#7) helped Boston bring home the Stanley Cup.

Orr's accomplishments almost defied logic. He won the Calder Trophy as rookie of the year in 1967. He won the James Norris Memorial Trophy as the league's outstanding defenseman an unprecedented eight times. He was selected winner of the Hart Trophy as the most valuable player three straight years, from 1970 to 1972. In 1970 he became the first defenseman ever to lead the league in scoring, and he captured the scoring title again in 1975. Also in 1970, Orr became the first player in history to capture four of the NHL's major individual awards in one season: the Hart Trophy, the Norris

Trophy, the Art Ross Trophy as scoring leader and the Conn Smythe Trophy as most valuable player in the playoffs.

Orr's presence, plus a series of shrewd managerial moves to add other top-notch players, transformed the Bruins into a championship contender. The Bruins' acquisition of center Phil Esposito from the Chicago Blackhawks was a stroke of genius. Boston general manager Milt Schmidt sent Gilles Marotte, Jack Norris and Pit Martin to Chicago for Esposito, Ken Hodge and Fred Stanfield. It turned out to be one of the most lopsided trades in hockey history and helped the Bruins win two Stanley Cups.

Esposito was a large, powerful center who camped in the slot area in front of opposing goals and made life miserable for defensemen and goaltenders. In Chicago he had played center on a line with superstar left wing Bobby Hull. Although Esposito set up many of Hull's goals, the attention usually went to Hull. In Boston, Esposito was out from behind Hull's shadow and became a superstar in his own right. In time, he replaced Hull, his former teammate, as the NHL's most dangerous goal scorer. In the 1970–71 season, Esposito scored 76 goals, which was the most anybody had scored up to that time.

Orr and Esposito were complemented by other top players, such as goaltender Gerry Cheevers; forwards Johnny Bucyk, Derek Sanderson and Johnny "Pieface" McKenzie; Esposito's linemates, Wayne Cashman and Ken Hodge; and sturdy defensemen Rick Smith, Don Awrey, Gary Doak and Dallas Smith. The Bruins were a big, bruising team. They intimidated their opponents with their ferocity, then defeated them with skill and style.

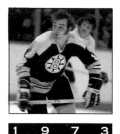

1 9 7 3

Ken Hodge chalked up eight goals during a seven-game scoring streak.

Phil Esposito had five straight 50-or-more goal seasons.

The 1969 playoffs showed what these new Bruins were all about. In the opening round against Toronto, Boston unleashed all its awesome goal-scoring power to rout the Maple Leafs 11-0 and 7-0 in the first two games and easily advanced.

The next round was against Montreal, the most successful team in league history and the hallmark by which all great hockey teams are measured. What resulted was a classic series. The Canadiens rallied to take the first two games on their home ice at the Montreal Forum, winning both in overtime. The Bruins refused to give up. They returned home to their noisy, boisterous crowd at Boston Garden and won the next two games to even the series. However, Montreal regrouped and won the next two games to capture the series en route to its second straight Stanley Cup and fourth in five years.

The Bruins learned from the experience and vowed it would be different in 1970. It was. They piled up 99 points during the regular season and were as ready as could be when the playoffs started. The biggest tests came early, against the New York Rangers and Chicago Blackhawks. The Bruins defeated the Rangers in a six-game series. Then, despite playing the first two games in Chicago, they swept the Blackhawks to advance to the finals. But this time they didn't have to deal with the Canadiens. Instead, the opponent was St. Louis, one of six teams from the NHL's expansion of three seasons before.

The 1970 final series began in St. Louis with the Bruins winning two straight. A victory in Game 3 in Boston set up the clincher. Veteran left wing Johnny Bucyk sent Game 4 into overtime with a goal late in the third period. Then, with the pre-

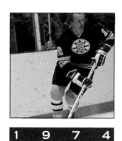

1 9 7 4

Left wing Wayne Cashman was named to the Second Team All-Stars.

Left to right: Stan Jonathan, Mike Milbury, Terry O'Reilly, Gerry Cheevers.

cision of a laser beam, Derek Sanderson set up Orr for the memorable Stanley Cup–winning goal in overtime, and the Bruins had won the Stanley Cup for the first time in 29 years.

"I never thought there could be such a day," Orr said. "This is what every kid dreams of, scoring the winning goal in a Stanley Cup overtime final. Wow. I can't find words to express what I feel." Coach Harry Sinden said, "I couldn't have written a better script. The kid has been tremendous . . . he shows me a new trick every game and never ceases to amaze me.

"We have talent, spirit, harmony and an unquenchable thirst for victory. What more could a coach ask?"

The Stanley Cup success elevated the Bruins to the next level. Some people around the league were even calling the Bruins the best team they had ever seen and stacking up the Boston lineup—Orr, Esposito, Bucyk and the rest—against the great teams of the past. However, a long-standing Montreal jinx continued. After romping through the regular season with a club-record 121 points, the Bruins stumbled in the 1971 playoffs. They lost a seven-game quarterfinal series to the Canadiens.

The Bruins atoned in 1972 by winning their second Stanley Cup in three seasons. They finished first in the Eastern Division, then romped past Toronto and St. Louis and finally the New York Rangers in an outstanding final series.

But with Orr skating on scarred knees—he underwent five knee operations during his career—the Bruins could not extend their dominance beyond the two championships. His injuries forced Orr into a premature retirement. He left the Bruins after the 1975–76 season as the most honored defenseman in history.

1 9 7 6

Gilles Gilbert won 17 straight games, a club record for the longest win streak by a goaltender.

Rick Middleton is among the all-time leaders in scoring (pages 26-27).

Milt Schmidt remarked: "If anybody greater ever comes along in the future, I just hope the Good Lord lets me stick around to see him."

Don Cherry coached the Bruins to the Stanley Cup finals, but the team lost to Montreal.

BEHIND THE BENCH: DON CHERRY

A natty, outspoken Canadian took over as coach of the Bruins in the 1974–75 season. Don Cherry (whose nickname, ironically, was "Grapes") was a career minor leaguer who wore double-breasted suits, wild ties and huge collars on his dress shirts. His brand of hockey was rough-and-tumble and his coaching style boisterous and dramatic. He was a perfect fit in Boston, where the Bruins continued to play the kind of aggressive hockey that had become the trademark style of the Big, Bad Bruins. "The fans love aggressive hockey," Cherry said.

Cherry had the team suited to play grinding hockey, with players such as Stan Jonathan, Mike Milbury, John Wensink, Carol Vadnais and Terry O'Reilly, whose Irish ancestry and physical style of play made him the prototype Bruin. Cherry and Harry Sinden, coach of the 1970 championship team who was now general manager, surrounded them with highly skilled players such as Jean Ratelle, Brad Park and Rick Middleton.

In Cherry's five seasons behind the bench, from 1974 through 1979, the Bruins were as good as any team in the league, but couldn't win the Stanley Cup. It was the timing. First they ran into the Philadelphia Flyers' two straight championships, then still another Montreal dynasty came along to capture the Cup four straight years through 1979. In three of those seasons the Bruins were eliminated from the playoffs by a very strong Canadiens squad.

Following the 1978–79 season, the Bruins released Cherry, citing philosophical differences on his handling of players. "They thought I was too close to the players," said Cherry, who went on to stardom as a television commentator. To this day he speaks fondly of his beloved Bruins. "Boston was my town," he said. "The Bruins will always be special."

THE TRADITION CONTINUES

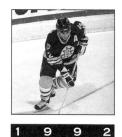

1 9 9 2

Adam Oates led the Bruins in scoring with 45 goals and 97 assists.

The Bruins remain one of hockey's premier clubs, perpetuating the tradition behind Harry Sinden's keen insights and ability to replenish the roster with Bruins-type players. In the past decade, Sinden has acquired in trades such star-quality players as goaltender Andy Moog and forwards Cam Neely, Adam Oates and Dave Poulin, all major contributors.

There is another reason the Bruins have flourished in the 1980s and 1990s. His name is Raymond Bourque and, like Shore and Orr before him, he is the best defenseman of his day.

The Bruins selected Bourque in the first round, eighth overall, of the 1979 NHL draft. From the very first moment he skated onto the ice at Boston Garden, Bourque has given the Bruins outstanding play and leadership. He was rookie of the year in 1980, has won the Norris Trophy as the league's outstanding defenseman five times and has been an All-Star in each of his 15 seasons. There is an irony to Bourque wearing a Boston uniform. He is a native of Montreal and grew up as a great fan of the Canadiens, the rivals that have caused the Bruins so much misery over the years.

Bourque is the ultimate two-way defenseman, combining excellent offensive skills with a solid defensive game. Hockey

Ray Bourque has a record number of All-Star Team honors.

In 1991, Cam Neely was the No.2 NHL goal scorer.   31

fans have come to expect as much from any player considered the Bruins' finest defenseman.

Through the years the Bruins have been a reflection of the city they represent, a burly, boisterous collection of players who deserve their reputation as the Big, Bad Bruins. They prefer to skate in a straight line, going over opposing players instead of around them. There is nothing subtle about their style. It is simple, but effective. Not only has it earned them the loyalty of the Boston fans, but it has made the Bruins one of the most attractive road draws in the NHL.

From Eddie Shore to Bobby Orr to Raymond Bourque, the Boston Bruins always have been, and will continue to be, a team with a special place in hockey history.

1 9 9 5

Dave Reid continues to be a consistent performer as he enters his twelfth season of NHL play.